EVERYONE IS A
LEADER

FIFTY PRACTICAL WAYS TO BUILD
TOMORROW'S LEADERS TODAY

HAMP LEE III

(com)mission
PUBLISHING

MONTGOMERY, ALABAMA

Recommendations within *Everyone Is a Leader: Fifty Practical Ways to Build Tomorrow's Leaders Today* are for informational and educational purposes only. Please consult with the appropriate (and respective) professionals, agencies, or groups before acting on the information in this book.

Cover photo by Pearl.

Everyone Is a Leader: 50 Practical Ways to Build Tomorrow's Leaders Today
Hamp Lee III -- 1st ed.

Library of Congress Control Number: 2016913364
ISBN 978-1-940042-34-3

TABLE OF CONTENTS

INTRODUCTION

Everyone is a leader. If you think about it, at some point in your life, you've been given the responsibility of leadership. From babysitting, leading a class project, working as a shift manager, to mowing lawns for extra candy money, you've served in some capacity of leadership.

Opportunities of leadership can occur anytime a person of higher authority or responsibility appoints you to a position to complete an assignment or task. This authority could have been your parents, teachers, coaches, and so on.

Some people believe leadership is easy stuff—just tell people what to do. However, leadership goes far beyond that. Leaders are expected to complete assigned tasks in a timely manner, embody organizational principles and values, manage people and resources responsibly, lead with integrity, and build cohesive, well-functioning teams toward specific and future goals. In order to meet these expectations, leaders will require the collection of many different traits, skills, and abilities—often at the same time.

Everyone Is a Leader: Fifty Practical Ways to Build Tomorrow's Leaders Today encompasses fifty leadership principles I believe are critical for developing effective leaders with good morals and sound character. As you read this book, consider it your leadership encyclopedia.

Just as an encyclopedia has an alphabetical listing of different subjects, *Everyone Is a Leader: Fifty Practical Ways to Build Tomorrow's Leaders Today* is structured in the same manner. As you read, you'll also find cross-references such as (36) that correspond to a chapter of a related subject in the book.

You don't have to read from chapter one to fifty, though I would recommend it for your first reading. You can skip to a subject in the middle of the book. Skim through it. Study it. Write all over it. This is *your* book to read, study, and share with others.

Everyone Is a Leader: Fifty Practical Ways to Build Tomorrow's Leaders Today was written from the perspective of the office environment; however, these principles are applicable to parents, students, church and community leaders, military members, sports teams, and others. You can exchange the office examples for whatever level or category of leadership that's applicable to you.

Thank you for allowing *Everyone Is a Leader: Fifty Practical Ways to Build Tomorrow's Leaders Today* to accompany you on your leadership journey. I hope this book becomes one of your sources for developing into the leader you always hoped to be.

O N E

100

One hundred is a number we often associate with completion, being full, and nothing lacking. For those taking a test, it's a sign of absolute mastery of a subject or task. If exercising or playing a sport, it refers to the level of effort expended. In friendship, it's the ultimate level of dedication to and support of another person. In leadership, one hundred encompasses them all.

As a leader, you want to have a *one hundred* attitude. If you're going to speak, give 100 percent of yourself to your audience. If you're going to support something, give 100 percent. When listening to others, be completely engaged and attentive.

A *one hundred* attitude is something no one can give or take away from you. It's something you decide to give every day; to everything you do. It sets the tone for how you approach every task and those you lead.

You can't expect *one hundred* from your followers if you intentionally give less. Lead by example.

One hundred is more than a number. It's a way of thinking...a way of life.

LEADERSHIP REFLECTION

Do you believe you give *one hundred* at home, work, and in your community? If not, please explain why.

In the areas you give *one hundred*, how have your efforts benefitted others?

In the areas you don't give *one hundred*, how has your personal and professional lives been impacted?

How can you improve the level of effort you give to your tasks, people, and organizations?

T W O
ACCOUNTABILITY

Accountability is inherent with leadership. It represents the personal and corporate responsibility for the actions and results of any delegated position and assignment, and every person and resource under said responsibility.

1. Personal accountability represents what you have direct control over—the things you say, do, and personally work on. This is the level of commitment and effort you give to your tasks, people, and organizations. No one can increase or decrease your level of commitment or effort. This is dependent on your own personal integrity. You have to decide whether you'll give *one hundred* or less (1).

2. Corporate accountability also represents what you have direct control over, but this relates to your followers and the tasks you assign them (6). You have less control over the results because the completion of each task (you're ultimately responsible for) depends on your followers' personal accountability.

When it comes to corporate accountability, and things don't go as planned, it's important for you to take responsibility for what occurs. As the leader, you're accountable for your team's failures. Though one of your followers might be directly responsible for the outcome, address the matter internally, while corporately accepting responsibility. Don't run to your superiors blaming followers for the mistakes of your team. That's not a sign of leadership, but rather, someone unwilling to be accountable for his or her area of responsibility—which reflects poorly on you as a leader.

LEADERSHIP REFLECTION

Describe your personal and corporate responsibilities—for example, supervisor, parent, program manager, etc.

Consider one or two of your most successful (and not so successful) leadership experiences. What factors did personal and corporate accountability have in your success or failure? What would you have done differently, if anything?

How can you show greater personal and corporate accountability?

T H R E E
ADVERSITY

If you're in a position of leadership, sooner or later, you'll experience some type of adversity. I'm not saying mobs of people will come after you with pitchforks and torches, but someone or something will confront you and challenge your decisions, leadership, and/or the programs, people, and organizations you lead.

When adversity comes to your doorstep, a decision to freeze, take flight, or fight can make the difference in your ability to appropriately address, resolve, and weather adverse situations.

1. Freeze. Adversity can be ugly, messy, and nasty. It can destroy the best of situations, relationships, and opportunities for you and your team. If you're honest with yourself, sometimes you'd rather avoid adversity at all costs, hoping it'll go away with time. So you do nothing.

Leaders freeze for a number of reasons. Some freeze because they don't know what to do and are overwhelmed by their circumstances. Some are scared of making the wrong decision, so they make no decision. Others freeze because they don't like confrontation.

However, not all adverse situations can be resolved by doing nothing. Leaving adversity unchecked can create deeper and more challenging problems for you and everyone involved.

2. Flight. Some leaders run from adverse situations for many of the same reasons as leaders who freeze. The difference is that in flight, they often make a conscious decision to mentally, emotionally, or physically run from adversity. What this amounts to is the leader refusing to uphold his or her responsibility to face issues and entities seeking to interrupt his or her effectiveness.

There are also times when flight is the most appropriate response because of personal temptations or hazardous conditions, for example.

3. Fight. In fight, you decide to face the adversity in spite of your fear, uncertainty, or desire to freeze or run. You attempt to resolve the issue regardless of the probability of a successful outcome. You *fight* because you believe it's the right thing to do.

Adverse situations can be emotional and very difficult to address. At varying points, you'll need mental toughness, perseverance, and good problem-solving skills (25, 35, 39). Though adversity can be a messy business, on the flip side, when appropriate, facing adversity can provide opportunities for growth, innovation, and success.

LEADERSHIP REFLECTION

Describe your greatest test or challenge of adversity.

Share a time when you grew personally or professionally as a result of facing an adverse situation. Describe the circumstances surrounding the event.

What is the most important lesson you've learned from adversity?

F O U R
ANGER

Leadership will provide many *opportunities* for you to become angry. People will use your name in vain, mistreat you, take advantage of you, and spread every slanderous lie possible. You might feel an uncontrollable anger that burns deep inside you wanting to fight back, speak your mind, and avenge the wrong done to you. You want to see the person (or people) squirm, beg for mercy, and ask for forgiveness. You want everyone to know you're the *wrong person* to mess with and to think twice before they speak or act!

However, nothing good comes from allowing uncontrollable anger to fuel your behavior. Like throwing gasoline on a fire, this type of anger drives more impulsive and irrational decisions. You yell at innocent bystanders, separate friends and coworkers, and create hostile environments at home and work. No one in your path is safe.

Words and actions do not come with refunds or do-overs. Therefore, it'll be important for you to recognize when anger seeks to fuel your thoughts or cloud your decision-making. Have the courage (and humility) to pause, walk away, ask questions when you're calm again, seek wise counsel, and think rationally before responding (27). Find the best and most appropriate way to address your situation or circumstance. Sometimes silence is the best answer.

Now, there are times when anger is a good motivator. Let's say you witness some type of suffering or injustice. Instead of exercising uncontrollable anger, you decide to filter it so you can provide productive responses that encourage collaborative solutions.

Watch your anger. Remain mentally focused. Protect your heart. Guard your mouth. Keep your emotions in check.

LEADERSHIP REFLECTION

Describe the last time you allowed uncontrollable anger to get the best of you. How did you react? How did those around you respond? What was the result of your conduct? What could you have done differently?

Describe a time when you wanted to lash out in anger but chose an alternative solution. How did you react? How did those around you respond? What was the result of your approach?

How has the *appropriate* use of anger been a benefit to you, your team, or your organization?

F I V E
ASKING FOR PERMISSION OR FORGIVENESS

As a leader, you'll frequently be accountable to someone with greater positional authority. You'll often coordinate with him or her to collaborate, receive guidance, or gain approval to proceed with a specific task or function.

A situation might arise when you don't have the time or means to coordinate with your superior and must make a decision on his or her behalf. Because the decision might be time sensitive, you have to decide whether you're going to wait for permission to proceed or take action and ask for forgiveness later.

Asking for forgiveness simply means moving forward with a decision without first speaking to your superior. There are times when asking for forgiveness is appropriate and times when it's not. So before you consider taking action and asking for forgiveness later, you should have the following areas covered:

1. Understand your superior's direction and guidance. Some superiors will trust you to make a decision; others will not. Some would want you to defer back to him or her regardless of the sensitivity of the issue. You need to know what your superior's stance is on such matters.

2. Build trust (49). Being able to make a decision without your superior is based on trust. As you develop your working relationship and serve as a capable and effective follower, you might prove to your superior that you can be trusted to handle certain leadership decisions in his or her absence.

3. Count the cost of your decision. Because you are making a decision on behalf of your superior, you must understand not only the issue, but also how your decision impacts other connected areas and functions. Consult with other leaders, gather background information, talk with those directly involved, and don't be afraid to ask questions. Be thorough and well informed.

Don't be afraid to make a decision out of fear of being wrong. The decision you make is based on the information presented to you at that moment. A failure to act can be costly in certain circumstances.

4. Brief your superior as soon as possible. Provide all pertinent information to your superior on the decision you made. Some will want every imaginable detail, and others will only want the highlights (remember the first point). Address any takeaways and tasks that may have been assigned.

LEADERSHIP REFLECTION

Describe a time when you made a higher-level decision without first coordinating with your superior. Compare your example with the four areas provided in this chapter. What was the outcome? What could you have done differently, if anything?

S I X
ASSIGNMENTS

Leaders are often in the best position to assign responsibilities and tasks because they have (or can receive) the oversight, background information, and available personnel. Working in coordination with other functional leads and specialists, leaders should strive to assign the most qualified person to a responsibility or task.

Right person. Right time. Right place.

It's vitally important to assign the right person to the right position at the right time. Just because someone is available, it doesn't mean that individual can effectively accomplish a responsibility or task. So if the right person isn't available, should you go with the next available person? Well, it depends...

Will the reassignment be temporary or permanent?

Are there any additional skills or training required?

Will this person be required to maintain his or her previous responsibilities and tasks?

What impacts might arise as a result of the new responsibility or task?

You must ensure that you provide whomever you select for a responsibility or task with your direction, guidance, training, and resources to be successful in that new position. It's not enough to assign someone to a responsibility or task and then walk away expecting that person to be successful. You must communicate your expectations and provide the means for him or her to meet each one (14).

If you assign responsibilities or tasks not suited for specific individuals or align people and groups with conflicting personalities, you might create greater frustration and reduced productivity. However, the better you become at aligning the right people with the right responsibilities and tasks, the more you'll increase your leadership and organizational capabilities while providing greater opportunities for growth and development.

As you assign responsibilities or tasks, it'll be important for you to follow up with both the new member and office personnel throughout his or her orientation and assignment. Maintain an open dialogue with all affected parties. Allow each member to provide candid feedback on the move and any current or foreseeable issues or challenges. If any issues or challenges arise, address them quickly (39).

LEADERSHIP REFLECTION

Describe a situation when you were assigned a responsibility or task you were not suited for due to a lack of training, personnel, or resources. What was the final outcome? If the outcome was not positive, what could have been done differently?

Describe a situation when you assigned the right person to a responsibility or task but not at the right time or place. What was the final outcome?

What difficulties have you encountered when trying to find the right person for a responsibility or task?

S E V E N
ASSOCIATIONS

Associations can open doors of opportunity but can also slam many more in your face.

From our earliest moments in childhood, we associated with others who had similar aims or goals. Sometimes those goals were as simple as finding kids to play hide-and-seek, someone to ride bikes with around the neighborhood, or a study partner. Your needs often drove who you would associate with.

Say for example, you found a few neighborhood kids to ride bikes with. During one ride, your new friends stopped at the local store, walked in, stuffed candy bars in their pockets, and walked out. Though you might have been shocked and scared by what occurred, you never had any desire or felt any pressure to steal anything. You only wanted to ride bikes in your neighborhood. But because of your association with these kids, three things could have happened:

1. You could have been encouraged or pressured to steal.

2. People might have believed you also stole candy bars because of your association with these kids.

3. If caught, you could have received the same punishment because you were in the wrong place at the wrong time with the wrong people.

As another example, Jack, a graphic designer, would like to work at a larger firm. His friend Brian works at a larger firm as a department manager. Jack has been playing soccer with Brian for the last three years in a community league. Jack speaks to Brian about his desire to work at the company and asks if he can put in a *good* word for him. This seems like a simple request, but let's consider two scenarios:

1. Because Brian is well respected at the firm, his recommendations carry a lot of weight. Though Brian questions Jack's work ethic and conduct on and off the soccer field, he provides a strong recommendation to the hiring official anyway. Jack is hired within a few weeks but is fired after a few months because of a lack of performance and misconduct. Now Brian's judgment is under scrutiny because he recommended Jack.

2. Brian is not well liked at the firm. His performance (and that of his team) is mediocre at best. Brian's recommendation may not carry a lot of weight, but at Jack's request, Brian sends his recommendation to the hiring official. Now Jack's reputation is in question because of his association with Brian.

Often, it's not what you know; it's who you associate with.

Take time to inventory your associations and determine whether you should remain connected to specific people or organizations. Just as you can use your associations to potentially receive a specific benefit or advantage, others can do the same using their association with you.

LEADERSHIP REFLECTION

Provide an example of an association that was positive and another that was (potentially) harmful or negative.

Describe the last time you used an association to receive a specific benefit or advantage.

E I G H T
ATTENTION TO DETAIL

It's all about the details.

When I was young, my grandmother had a pink figurine of a boy sitting on a toilet. A caption next to the boy read, "The job isn't finished until the paperwork is done." There's a literal meaning for the figurine, but in leadership, there are many details you must consider with each job, task, and assignment you're given. Some details will improve your final product and others will enhance your performance. But no matter what you're assigned to do, it's important to get the details right.

Attention to detail represents those things that show that you and your team know what you're doing and care about what you're doing. It shows your level of commitment, dedication, and effort to your craft in order to make the good...great.

Anyone can show attention to detail. Some jobs, tasks, and assignments will come easier to some than others, but each person can be detail-oriented. To display greater attention to detail, you'll need three things: personal pride, a commitment to learning, and a willingness to see a job, task, or assignment through completely.

1. Personal pride. In each job, task, or assignment, you represent yourself, your family name, and every organization you belong to (22). When you display personal pride, you intentionally provide your best effort and focus. Whether the world sees your effort or walks right past it without a single glance, you give each job, task, and assignment 100 percent because your name is associated with it (1).

2. Commitment to learning. In order to pay attention to detail, you must know what you're doing. This is a sign of competence (and mastery) of your job, task, or assignment. Through reading, asking questions from competent authorities, and a bit of hands-on experience, you can increase your knowledge and skill (31). As your competency improves, you'll have the ability to see and understand how you can improve your work.

3. Willingness to see a job through completely. This goes back to my grandmother's pink figurine—making sure the paperwork is done. It's the little things that take your job, task, or assignment to the next level.

Paying attention to detail is something you should incorporate into everything you do. Allow attention to detail to become a way of life—a standard of conduct. When you create this standard of living, you have the potential to create a culture of excellence at home, work, and in every organization you lead.

If you don't pay attention to detail in places like your organization, your actions will also create a specific culture. Your followers will know they can cut corners and give less effort and focus because you won't have the personal pride, knowledge, or commitment to know the difference. And if you try to demand attention to detail from your followers when you don't exercise it yourself, you may be viewed as a hypocrite and lose your credibility and influence as their leader. "Do as I say, not as I do" doesn't work. Lead by example.

Though showing attention to detail is a cost of your time and effort, the benefits are exponentially larger. You'll establish your identity as a leader, set the tone for your team and organization, and potentially open new doors for greater roles and opportunities.

LEADERSHIP REFLECTION

Share an example of when you've shown attention to detail in your job, task, or assignment. What made your level of detail stand out from other jobs, tasks, or assignments?

Describe any obstacles or challenges you faced when trying to show attention to detail in your jobs, tasks, and assignments. How did you overcome them?

N I N E
AUTHORITY

Authority is the legitimate or perceived use of power or ability one has over a task or group of people. It's often given, passed down, delegated, or assumed from one person or group to another.

Legitimate Authority

Legitimate authority is the actual issuance, delegation, or relinquishing of power to another person. He or she receives all inherent rights, permissions, and responsibilities associated with the position or assignment and has the means to take full ownership and accountability over its direction, maintenance, and care (2).

Perceived Authority

Perceived authority represents the authority members of a group give to another person within the group without official approval or recognition from the leader with legitimate authority. Often through his or her social connections, character, or charisma, he or she is considered an unofficial leader who has a specific level of influence over the other group members.

Addressing Members with Perceived Authority

Though group members with perceived authority don't have the legitimate authority you carry, they're influential gatekeepers. Therefore, it's extremely important that you identify these individuals within your group. You must understand how they can affect or have affected your ability to effectively lead and provide influential counsel in completing team assignments. Based on their motives, you might face many challenges in successfully leading your group.

Regardless of whether the actions of these individuals have been beneficial to your group, you must keep a close eye on your group dynamic. Your other group members have given them some level of influence over their decisions and behavior. Therefore, ensure your group doesn't become something you never intended.

There are three ways you can address members in your group with perceived authority. Each method can have positive or negative effects on your group dynamic and should be carefully considered before deciding on a course of action.

1. Establish your authority by force. This method is the most direct, but can be the most disruptive to your group. You confront this member and let him or her know you're in charge and define what he or she will no longer be

permitted to say or do within the group. He or she might comply with your request and become a team player, but more often, you'll experience a second reaction—rebellion.

Your direct confrontation might be a *blow* to his or her ego because you're trying to take away something that person cherishes—power and influence. He or she might be hurt, angry, and unwilling to relinquish his or her position. Now you have a fight on your hands for control of *your* group. In more extreme examples, the individual will use his or her influence to reduce your influence or destroy the entire group dynamic just to keep his or her perceived authority.

2. Together Everyone Achieves More (TEAM). You can choose to be more of a team player and work with the member with perceived authority. Like a coach with a team of players, each member has different talents, gifts, and personalities. The coach takes these individual players and finds ways to bring them together as a cohesive team. He or she maximizes each player's skill set to deliver a winning formula for each one to share and celebrate together. You can do the same as a leader among your group.

Even among teammates, there are team captains and other informal leaders. Coaches identify these individuals as an extension of the team's development and leadership. And though you did not appoint these members, you can use them as integral extensions of your leadership to help you build a successful and cohesive group. But remember to remain vigilant and watchful.

3. Remove the member from the group. Regardless of what you say or do, some members with perceived authority will prove too toxic or detrimental to the growth and success of your group. The best and only decision you might have is removing the member.

Like pulling on a spider web, many people might be connected to that member when you try to remove him or her from your group. You must carefully consider your plan for removing this member, as you don't want to negatively impact your group dynamic with his or her departure (remember the first point). If you're running a business or organization, you should also seek legal counsel to ensure any termination or other course of action is well within established limits.

Another way of removing this member is to find him or her a new opportunity (6). New opportunities can provide a change of scenery that brings fresh vigor and ideas for both the group and the member. However, be considerate of the opportunities you're considering. You want to find the best fit for the member and the organization.

Lastly, communicate your desires to the member upfront. Don't allow this person to be the last to know. He or she might learn of your intentions through another source, and rumors could become his or her truth. However, no matter what you attempt to do, some members will not take news of their removal well. Remember to consider the member's thoughts, emotions, and experiences (16, 47).

Whether you have legitimate or perceived authority, you must understand the full measure of responsibility given to you. At its core, other people trust your opinions and leadership to help them and the group or organization succeed (49). They're depending on you to uphold your position of authority with the utmost honesty and integrity (30).

You've been given a sacred trust to lead and serve your team and organization effectively. Any abuse of authority, no matter how small, can greatly interfere with your effectiveness to lead. Careless words and actions, abusing your authority, hidden agendas, inciting division and strife, and disrespecting your superiors are surefire ways to lose your credibility, authority, and influence. Teams and organizations can be ripped apart because of your actions, leaving you with neither legitimate or perceived authority.

LEADERSHIP REFLECTION

Share a personal example of someone who abused his or her legitimate or perceived authority. How did that person's actions impact the group? What was the end result? What did the situation teach you about authority in leadership?

How can someone with perceived authority positively or negatively impact your team and group dynamic?

T E N
BALANCE

Maintaining a balanced life is a delicate art. Each day can be filled with so many tasks, responsibilities, and decisions that you often feel like you're being pulled in several directions at once. You wish you could add a twenty-fifth hour to the day, but even that might not be enough.

With a finite amount of time and energy, you only have so much of yourself you can give to accomplish everything you (and others) want, need, or desire. If you give too much, you run the risk of experiencing conditions that lead to burnout and exhaustion.

Burnout and exhaustion create blind spots when it comes to the true condition of your physical, mental, social, and spiritual health (25). Destructive behaviors can manifest where you become less attentive or begin to act out of character by doing and saying things you normally wouldn't, lowering your personal standards and boundaries (46).

Before you experience any imbalance, it's important to regularly inventory the major areas of your life. One of the ways you can inventory how you balance these areas is through a RESET.

RESET

To reset something is to set again or differently. A RESET in this context, is a planned review of the major areas of your life in order to maintain balance and prevent burnout and exhaustion.

Based on your schedule, you can choose a daily, weekly, or monthly RESET. You want to establish an interval that provides a bit of space between reviews in order to identify certain behaviors and issues before they can grow into major problems (11).

In your review, write down the major areas of your life, such as work, family, personal time, exercise, fellowship, and community service. After identifying these areas, please consider the following questions:

On a scale of 1–10 (1 = poor, 10 = ideal), how would you rate your balance in each of your major areas?

Were there any areas that received more of your attention or energy? If so, please explain why.

Have you overcommitted yourself in one or more areas? If so, please explain how.

Have you ever become frustrated or angry because of an imbalance in one or more areas? If so, please describe your frustrations.

Has stress or an imbalance in any area created negative habits (overeating, inappropriate comments or relationships, for example)? If so, please explain.

As you gain greater awareness of the major areas of your life that may be out of balance, describe what you might need to add or remove in order to gain greater balance. Consider who you might need to speak to, questions you might need to ask, any necessary coordination, and tough decisions to ponder.

When adding or removing specific items from your life, you should also establish standards and boundaries (46). These necessary guards protect your time, health, and energy so you can be productive and effective (48). However, this isn't always easy.

Knowing you need to make a change and doing something about it are two separate issues. You can talk, plan, and review all day long, but as long as you do that, your life remains the same...and in danger of becoming worse.

Change doesn't come by thinking about it. It comes by acting on it.

As you execute your plan to maintain balance, it's important to continually review your status (until your next RESET) to ensure you remain on the right path. Don't become so distracted by your needs, wants, and desires that maintaining balance becomes an afterthought. If you don't take time to continually inventory your tasks, responsibilities, and decisions, you might watch your effectiveness dwindle, projects remain incomplete, opportunities be lost, and relationships fade because of imbalance.

LEADERSHIP REFLECTION

What is your current interval for completing your RESET? Daily? Weekly? Monthly?

Have you placed your RESETs on your calendar or smartphone as a reminder?

What benefit(s) have you experienced from establishing a RESET?

As you gain greater balance in your life, are you also creating an environment that allows your followers to do the same?

From the items or areas you identified that can (or should) be removed from your life, which would be the hardest to extract? Please explain.

As you consider items or areas to extract, what items or areas should be added or increased in order to bring greater balance in your life?

E L E V E N
BREAKING GLASS

In most public buildings, you'll find small red fire alarm boxes. Their levers are encased in glass with "In case of emergency, break glass" written on their outside frames. When the glass is broken and the lever is pulled, an alarm sounds, and the fire department is notified.

Around you every day are situations that start as small embers but can grow into massive fires (problems) if not properly addressed. There are some situations you can't anticipate or control, but there are many others well within your control to prevent. Therefore, it'll be important for you to find the *smoke*, extinguish it, and build safeguards.

Find the Smoke

In leadership, you'll experience interpersonal issues, product inefficiencies, reduced resources, and failures of character or conduct. Before these issues can become significant problems, you'll have to take the initiative to seek them out in their infancy or address them as soon as you're notified.

Extinguish It

Properly gather and review the facts, interview all members involved, and seek out any necessary counsel and advice (19, 38). Some issues can be addressed over a short conversation or meeting. Other issues will require intricate coordination and participation.

Build Safeguards

As you resolve issues, implement procedures to ensure similar issues either don't occur again or can be easily (and quickly) identified (17, 38). Build consensus. Follow up. Remain vigilant. You never know where *smoke* might appear next.

LEADERSHIP REFLECTION

Describe a time when you saw a small problem in your area of responsibility and you didn't address it right away. What warning signs existed? What was the final outcome? What conclusions can be drawn from your example?

T W E L V E
CHARACTER

Character refers to the mental and moral qualities distinctive to an individual. It's the culmination of your interactions with the people and events around you based on your past experiences and decisions and inherited traits. Though this topic is twelfth in this book, a lapse in character is often the number-one reason why people descend from positions of leadership.

Your gifts, talents, intellect, and abilities can place you in the company of great people and present many opportunities. However, what few people often realize is that it's their character that can sustain, grow, or diminish their position and legacy.

Without a high standard of sound character, sooner or later, a lapse in character will surface that has the potential of destroying the reputation and legacy you spent so many years building. Even if you overcome your character flaws and receive another opportunity, you might continually live under the dark shadow of your previous indiscretions.

Having sound character is a priceless commodity. Every action, good or bad, is recorded in the hearts and minds of each person you interact with. How you project your character will speak volumes about your credibility, standing, and legacy as a leader.

LEADERSHIP REFLECTION

Describe the person who has the greatest personal character you know.

Share an example of how a lapse in character affected someone you know.

When confronted with a decision on whether to give someone with a previous lapse in character an opportunity for redemption, what decision did you make? What factors led to your decision? If you have yet to experience this, discuss what thoughts and actions could possibly be included in your decision.

When people mention your name, what do you think they say about you? What would you want them to say?

How do you want to be remembered? How can your character flaws get in the way of this?

T H I R T E E N
COLLABORATION

Collaboration is the process of working with an individual, group, or agency toward a specific and/or common goal or purpose. This goal of collaboration is developed through the sharing of ideas, gifts, talents, and resources to exponentially increase the impact and completion of any project or task that one person could accomplish on his or her own.

Collaboration is most effective through connections and communities formed through personal interactions. Personal interactions are the bedrock of collaboration as it encompasses a number of relationship-building principles that form the basis of a community with shared interests, abilities, and associations (7).

Connection

Connections are formed through personal and professional relationships based on shared interests, abilities, and associations. Some connections will expand beyond the initial interest or association and others will remain within the established relationship.

Community

Communities are established from personal and professional connections, but not all communities intermingle. For example, if you like to cook, you might be personally connected to other people that also likes to cook. Each person forms a community through his or her shared interest, yet will have other connections and communities separate from the cooking community. This allows your communities to become an interwoven fabric that shapes your connections and communities to expand your collaborative efforts toward a specific and/or common goal or purpose.

LEADERSHIP REFLECTION

Describe the last time you collaborated with another person or group. What were you seeking to accomplish? Illustrate the connections and communities that were involved. What was the final outcome?

Provide an example of a *benefit* you personally received through collaboration.

F O U R T E E N
COMMUNICATION

Communication is the foundation of leadership functions and operations. It is the transfer of information from one person to another in order to direct, persuade, inspire, correct, or simply inform. Because of its importance, information should be transmitted in a manner that can be received, understood, and acted upon as originally intended. This requires leaders to be strategic in what they say and how they say it. They do this by considering the sender, the receiver, and the message.

The Sender

The sender has very important responsibilities in communication. The sender must consider what needs to be communicated (*the what*), how he or she will communicate it (*the how*), and the assurance that the message is received as he or she originally intended (*the win*).

The sender must also address any biases he or she has with the message or the audience. If there is a message or audience that challenges the sender's beliefs, team goals, etc., he or she might be tempted to manipulate the message or its delivery to the detriment of its original intent.

The Message

In determining *the what*, it's important that the sender fully understands the message to be communicated. If he or she does not understand the message, its delivery and acceptance can be misinterpreted or dismissed.

In getting to *the how* of a sender's message, the method or delivery can vary based on time constraints, the knowledge and experience level of the audience, and the sender's purpose and intent. If a sender has information that is not critical or time sensitive, maybe an e-mail will suffice. When he or she wants to provide more of a personal touch, maybe a handwritten note would be best (36). There are pros and cons for each communication medium, so the sender must carefully consider how the message would be best conveyed.

The Receiver

Understanding the audience is important to the message a sender shares. A message to a group of ten-year-olds will differ from a discussion with college professors. Based on the audience, a sender's message might need to be brief, filled with references, or include some type of multimedia to enhance its delivery.

Once the sender speaks, presses send on an e-mail, or mails a letter, he or she has no control over how that message is perceived. Senders cannot assume each audience member will receive the message as they intended. Each person has his or her own perspective based on past experiences, convictions, and desires. And this is where *the win* comes in.

The win represents the receipt of a message as the sender originally intended. Now, the evidence of proper receipt is the accuracy of the receiver's actions. However, based on the information one shares, this might not be immediately possible or feasible, so the sender should go to the next best thing: follow-up.

In this instance, follow-up is the affirmative verification of the sender's message. Follow-up can be as simple as asking questions of the receiver, providing a summary of the information provided, or using some other method to ensure the message was properly understood as the sender originally intended. One of the most preferred methods might be direct person-to-person communication, such as face-to-face dialogue or telephone conversation. Person-to-person communication allows senders and receivers to ask specific questions, receive immediate answers or clarification, and share additional information and guidance.

LEADERSHIP REFLECTION

Have you ever shared a message that wasn't understood as you originally intended? Describe the factors involved with the miscommunication.

Was there ever a time when certain personal biases affected a message you shared with your audience? If so, please explain.

Outside of the information shared in this chapter, please share other important aspects of communication.

When has follow-up been an integral part of your communication?

F I F T E E N
COMPASSION

Compassion is the secret sauce of leadership.

The simplest definition of compassion is the outpouring of emotions, thoughts, and actions toward another person. This outpouring is presented as an offering of one's time, talent, resources, or money—without cost or strings attached (26).

Compassion is often motivated by emotions, not by uncontrollable anger or naïveté, but one of well-thought and well-placed intentions. Such thoughts and intentions become the motivation (and inspiration) to help someone, provide solutions, and help ease the pain and concern of others.

Expressions of compassion are not about winning awards or being recognized for good deeds and efforts. Compassion is helping another person become his or her best self.

You should never forget those days when you needed a handout, a little financial assistance, or a second (third, fourth, or fiftieth) chance. Never forget your days of humble beginnings; those days when you desperately needed someone to show compassion toward you, your family, or someone close to you (47).

There are people around you right now that are in need of compassion. They need to be encouraged, clothed, fed, provided shelter, or given a shoulder to cry on. And the investment you can make in their lives will often cost you a small bit of your time, talent, resources, or money, but it's in that small investment that can make a huge difference for someone in need (26).

Your legacy is not only built on the goals you achieve and products you create but the manner in which you touch the heart of another person.

LEADERSHIP REFLECTION

When was the last time you were motivated to help someone in need? Share your feelings and the outcome of your motivation.

Share a moment when someone showed compassion toward you. How did his or her actions impact you?

S I X T E E N
CONSIDERATION

Consideration is showing genuine concern and interest for the well-being of another person—whether the person is inside or outside your sphere of influence. It means you care about how people feel, how you make them feel, and how you can make their lives a little easier and more enjoyable.

You care whether your subordinates have the proper materials and equipment.

You care that department store workers don't have to roam the parking lot looking for your cart because you took the time to place it in the cart stall.

You care enough to give your seat to a pregnant woman on a crowded bus.

You care about another person's belongings as if they were your own.

You care about your impact on the people, organizations, and environment around you.

As a leader, your bottom line cannot solely be on production and mission accomplishment. When there's a lack of consideration for others, you might forget that people are human. They have problems and hard days. They make mistakes. They're doing the best they can with what they have. And maybe the consideration you show can make their day just a little easier.

LEADERSHIP REFLECTION

Was there ever a time when a leader was not considerate of your time, talent, resources, or money? How did his or her actions make you feel? How was your family or personal life affected?

What challenges have you experienced as a leader when considering another person's time, talent, resources, or money? Have you been tempted to ignore these concerns? If so, why...and what was the outcome?

Describe a situation when your consideration benefitted another person.

S E V E N T E E N
CONTINUITY

Continuity provides a consistent record of operations, standards, and procedures for a specific project or position within an organization. It provides historical information to reduce the time it takes for personnel to acclimate to a position or task. Continuity also reduces the duplication of work and effort while preventing reoccurring mistakes and unnecessary actions.

Because each person in your group and organization (including you) is replaceable, you should collaborate with your managers and supervisors on a plan for building continuity in your area of responsibility (13). Discuss what information should be captured, templates and medium to use, accessible locations to store your continuity, milestones and timelines for completion, and the creation of backup copies in case of loss, theft, or human-made or natural disasters.

Allow continuity building to be incorporated into your group's assigned responsibilities with the support and concurrence of your managers and supervisors. This will ensure there are no major interruptions in the event of an absence or departure.

LEADERSHIP REFLECTION

When has continuity been beneficial for a project or position in your area of responsibility?

Describe a situation when you needed continuity but didn't have it.

Do you have continuity for the projects and positions in your organization? If you don't, consider what steps you'll need to take to place a greater emphasis on developing continuity. Discuss other advantages and challenges you might foresee.

E I G H T E E N
CORRECTION

Correction is an important aspect of leadership. Correction helps to redirect thoughts, actions, and character traits toward an established or desired objective. The most important part of correction is establishing standards of performance and conduct.

Your followers must first know what's expected of them: acceptable rules of behavior, proper safety procedures, and office workflows, for example. Your standards must be provided and communicated upon hiring and in regular intervals throughout a follower's employment or service to ensure he or she is aware of the expectations, performance standards, and conduct as a member of your team and organization.

Rules of Understanding and Engagement

1. People don't like being corrected. Many people see correction as an attack on their persona, pride, or position. Understand that any *pushback* you receive might be more about their inability to accept correction with humility and maturity than the topic at hand (27).

2. Correction might contradict a person's perception of him- or herself. Many people have a high perception of themselves and will often fight (sometimes literally) to defend that perception, even if they know they're wrong.

These individuals might argue with you, ignore your correction, and find other ways to get you to see things their way. However, it's very important that you don't give in to their *games* or have a lapse of character because of your frustrations (12).

3. Address the matter quickly. Bad news doesn't change if you wait a day or two or become uncomfortable with confrontation. Use the most effective method based on your character, leadership style, and circumstances (14).

4. Create the right setting for correction. Because of the sensitive nature of correction, be considerate of where and how you correct others (16, 19, 39). As each person might respond differently to correction, your approach should be complementary to the person and situation.

5. Be truthful. Make sure you do your homework and have your facts straight before correcting others. Don't lie about specific details because you don't know the whole story. This will only break down your credibility, trust, and ability to provide effective correction.

6. Distance yourself emotionally. There's no need to respond to emotional chaos. Just stick to the facts and remain calm (4). Some people might start crying in front of you to motivate you to change your decision. Calmly

hand them a tissue box or ask them if they would like to go to the restroom to freshen up. Then ask them to return in order to continue (19).

7. Show humility (27). As my grandmother used to say, "don't show your natural tail." Don't be a jerk or act like a donkey because you're the boss and feel entitled to say whatever you want. Be considerate and sensitive to the thoughts, emotions, and lives of others, even if your correction is warranted (16). Treat others as you would want to be treated (47).

8. Exercise patience. Provide time and space for the person you corrected to process your message and appropriately address his or her own emotions and future decisions. The individual might not like what you say, but hopefully, he or she will come to respect you for it and improve.

Leadership is not a popularity contest. You're leading a group of people in a specific direction to accomplish specific tasks and assignments. Unfortunately, not everyone will behave like perfect little angels. People do get out of line from time to time and require correction. Your purpose in correction should help them reconsider their actions and refocus themselves so they can continue as integral members of your group and organization.

LEADERSHIP REFLECTION

What has been your most difficult challenge in accepting correction?

What has been your most difficult challenge in correcting others?

Describe a situation when you were corrected but didn't come to appreciate the correction until years later. Why were you initially apprehensive in accepting correction?

N I N E T E E N
COUNSELING

Counseling is the help and support in resolving personal, social, or psychological problems and difficulties, especially by a professional. As a leader, you'll often be looked upon to provide unbiased, thoughtful, and wise guidance; mediate difficult personnel issues; and listen to the concerns of your team, both large and small.

Counseling is not something you should take lightly. The advice you provide could change the direction of a person's life. Counseling should be approached with respect and care for each person involved. And as you provide your help and support, you must know when you've reached your limits of experience to provide effective counsel and refer him or her for professional help and assistance.

Requests for guidance or addressing issues and concerns shouldn't deter you from counseling others. As each person and situation you face will most likely be different, please consider the following eleven aspects of counseling:

1. Position but not permission. Not everyone will accept your counsel because of your position or authority. Even

when you provide the best possible solution, it doesn't guarantee he or she will accept your advice and act on it. There can be many issues or biases preventing a person from accepting your counsel. Sometimes only time, patience, and experience will be his or her teacher.

2. Be available. You should be visible and available to your followers. Establish an open-door policy where anyone can come to you. Allow your personnel to know where you are and how to get in contact with you if (and when) needed.

In order to be available, you'll also need to close off distractions (1). Be focused and engaged in the conversation. Don't drift mentally or spend time thinking about what you're going to say next. Turn off your television or computer monitor. Stop checking your phone or watch. Don't answer your phone (unless it's a legitimate emergency). Allow the person to believe that he or she is important to you and what he or she has to say matters.

3. Listen more; speak less. Sometimes a follower doesn't need a specific answer from you. Maybe he or she only needs someone willing to listen; an opportunity to vent or work through his or her thoughts to another person.

4. Get to the root. Issues are like trees. As trees have roots, there is a *root* for each problem you address. However, many leaders spend their time in counseling focused on the branches and leaves—symptoms of the root issue—rather than getting to the source. (Not all

symptoms should be ignored. Some symptoms have devastating consequences and must be addressed immediately.) Getting to the root of an issue can be a difficult and challenging endeavor, but it's one that can bring true resolution.

5. Ask open-ended questions. Open-ended questions can get a person thinking about varying perspectives of his or her issue. This allows for greater dialogue rather than yes-or-no answers.

6. Focus on one issue at one time. Trying to address multiple issues at once might not solve any issues. Less is more.

7. You cannot make someone believe what you believe...no matter how hard you try. Listen, share solutions, and allow the individual to come to his or her own conclusions. What might seem like an easy decision for you might not be as easy for someone else. If you try to force someone to believe what you do or to act on your advice, you may only cause greater frustration, and risk your ability to influence that person in the future.

8. Be patient. Change doesn't always occur right away. Plant a seed of information today, and wait for it to grow. Some seeds take a little longer than others. And as you wait, continue to be a source of constant and consistent support and advice.

9. Know when to stop or refer. There are times when a person has no intention of changing. There are also times

when you've reached the extent of your ability to provide effective counsel and believe another person or agency will be of greater assistance. When you believe the time is appropriate to refer the individual to another agency, share your concerns for additional assistance and be willing to accompany him or her. Continue to be supportive, visible, and available.

10. Conclude with an agreed plan of action. Before ending your discussion, provide a summary of your conversation and an action plan going forward. Be concise and specific.

11. Follow-up. People feel valued when they know you remembered them and care about their well-being. Follow-up establishes trust and solidifies personal connections. Follow-up also ensures the other person doesn't give up on his or her own path toward change. This keeps him or her *honest.*

LEADERSHIP REFLECTION

Has there ever been a time when someone tried to counsel you and you didn't listen to anything he or she said? What prevented you from accepting his or her advice? What biases existed? What was the final outcome of your situation?

What has been your greatest challenge in counseling others? Greatest success?

T W E N T Y
CREDIT

Give people credit where it's due...

Everyday, your followers give their time, talent, resources, and money to support you, your team, and your organization. For all the work and effort they put in, many of them only want to receive a thank-you, thumbs-up, pat on the back, or some other form of recognition. It's their way of feeling valued, validated, and appreciated. *Who better to give this than the leader?*

Acknowledging your team's hard work may not always come easy. As many tasks, responsibilities, and requirements fill your day, it'll be important for you to carve out time to show your followers how much you value and appreciate them—even if you need to spend your off-duty time to do so. These small sacrifices of your time will reap huge dividends from your team.

Provide meaningful and personalized recognition (36). Thank someone for a job well done or tell him or her how much you appreciate his or her efforts. Write award packages, memos of appreciation, and promotion recommendations, provide extra time off, or treat your team to a catered meal.

Create an environment where everyone in your area of responsibility knows that hard work and effort will not go unnoticed.

LEADERSHIP REFLECTION

How important has recognition been in your personal life and professional career?

Have you always been recognized for your hard work and efforts? If not, explain how you felt not to be recognized.

How does each member on your team like to be recognized?

What can you do to recognize your entire team?

EMPOWERMENT

Empowerment is the process of delegating a specific aspect of your authority to another person in order to accomplish a specific responsibility or task. Because you only have so much time, energy, and availability, empowerment gives you an opportunity to focus on meetings, projects, and decisions that are typically associated with your position as the leader while expanding other individual and organizational capabilities. It allows you and everyone on your team to become more effective and productive.

However, before you delegate any responsibility or task, please consider the following six aspects of empowerment:

1. Trust. When you empower your followers, you must be able to trust them to act in accordance with your guidance (5, 49). If you don't have confidence in their abilities, you might spend your valuable time micromanaging their efforts just to ensure you receive adequate support and effort.

2. Proper task assignment (6). Empowerment is not a haphazard assignment of responsibilities or tasks, but an

intentional alignment based on a follower's knowledge, skills, abilities, and personality in certain situations.

3. Communication (14). When empowering your followers, it's important that you share the right information in the right detail. When you communicate responsibilities and tasks, remember to address the who, what, when, where, why, and how. Based on the knowledge, skills, and abilities of those you're empowering, you might be more or less inclined to share greater information. However, you shouldn't assume these individuals know your exact deliverables. Communicate, communicate, communicate!

4. Inspiration. As you empower your followers, become a cheerleader for their success. It doesn't hurt to give a pat on the back or say how well a job is going. Give credit where it's due (20). Even if one of your followers misses the mark completely, use the opportunity as a teachable moment that inspires hope and encouragement.

5. Patience. Give your followers room to grow into the responsibility or task you've assigned. Allow them to make mistakes without fear of reprisal or removal. Continue to support them and show the same care and concern you wanted when you were in their position (47).

6. Follow up. As the leader, you're accountable for the responsibilities or tasks you assign others (2). Without micromanaging, schedule meetings at regular intervals to receive updates on their status and progress. Create an environment of open communication to address any strengths, weaknesses, opportunities, or obstacles.

LEADERSHIP REFLECTION

What benefit(s) have you found through empowerment?

What has been your most difficult aspect of empowering others?

How has patience played a role in empowering others?

Describe a situation when you were on a team and the leader did not empower you or the other team members. What was the outcome?

EXAMPLE

No matter where you are, you represent yourself, your family name, and every organization you belong to. In public and private settings, people are watching your example (40). Your mannerisms, speech, clothing, and interactions are being watched and scrutinized. They're watching how you treat people, your daily interactions, and what you do when you believe no one's looking. What they're looking for is a true leader. They want to see someone who lives up to what they believe a leader should be—a person they can trust, not someone they should stay far away from (49).

You can be the example you've always wanted to be. Each moment provides an opportunity to establish a positive example (12, 30). It's your chance to represent yourself, your family name, and your organizations well. The choice is yours to make...one decision at a time.

LEADERSHIP REFLECTION

What characteristics of a leader do you admire most?

Who has been the most inspiring or influential person in your life? Please explain how this person impacted you.

Take a moment to consider the example you're setting in public and private settings. How would the people around you be inspired or discouraged by your example?

What has been your most difficult challenge in being an example to others?

TWENTY - THREE
FORGIVENESS

Forgiveness is a personal decision to let go of any anger or resentment you hold because of an offense committed against you, someone you know, or a cause you hold dear. Though you can't control what someone might say or do, you can control how you respond.

There will be people you'll be able to forgive easier (or quicker) than others. Then there are others whose offenses create such deep wounds that it'll take a lot longer to reach a decision to forgive. Many people today have lived with unforgiveness for years. The wounds are so deep that their perspective on life and humanity as a whole might have been altered. This might affect how they maintain relationships, parent their children, and conduct daily business.

Now, in no way am I minimizing any act or event committed against you or anyone you know. There are people who experienced violent and heinous acts against them and have been traumatized through these events. These moments have left scars that might never heal.

Some scars the world sees, and others lie deep within, but forgiveness is about your freedom, your ability to live, lead, and love without limits, and to see the beauty of the world around you.

You might never forget an event that occurred in your life, but the emotional ties to that event does not have to keep you broken or incapable of moving forward. Your wounds and scars can heal. Freedom and peace can be yours again. You can discover life anew.

LEADERSHIP REFLECTION

How can unforgiveness affect your ability to lead others?

If you're comfortable, share a situation where you were struggling to forgive someone and the steps you took to reach a decision to forgive.

How would you respond to hearing you offended someone? Would you try to apologize and seek reconciliation or remain silent? What steps would you take to seek reconciliation, if any?

T W E N T Y - F O U R
GOSSIP

Gossip is a rumor or report of personal information, often of a sensational nature. Gossip can seem like the innocent sharing of information, but its intent isn't based on seeking solutions, help, or any other assistance.

When it comes to gossip, there are three things you should consider as a leader: whether you'll associate with gossipers, what you should do when you can't avoid a gossiper, and if you'll accept a gossiper's information as *your* truth.

As I mentioned previously, it's not what you know but who you associate with (7). You must give serious thought to whether you'll associate with gossipers. Your association with gossipers might give the perception of you being a gossiper, and for many people, perception is reality (34).

Trust is a valuable commodity for a leader, and your association with a gossiper could diminish the trust your followers have in you (49). Your followers want to know that if they say something to you in confidence, they won't hear it from someone else. If your followers can't trust you, a loss of loyalty and commitment could soon follow.

Now, there are times when you're unable to avoid associating with gossipers—at work or during community projects, for example. If you find yourself in such situations, please consider the following:

1. Never forget he or she is a gossiper. Gossipers present themselves as friendly, trustworthy, and faithful. They're often good listeners and provide shoulders to cry on, offer good advice, and have inviting personalities. This sets you up to lower your defenses and inhibitions while increasing your comfort level to share details of your life.

2. Establish clear boundaries (46). Having a working relationship doesn't require you to have a personal one. Handle business and move on. You don't have to be a jerk and treat them badly; just make sure you keep business as business and personal information to yourself. Don't stop to talk over coffee, chat in the hallway, or converse about anything outside of your shared business. As soon as your business is completed, politely excuse yourself.

3. Be cautious of what you share. Just assume that whatever you share with a gossiper will be shared with others. Don't share anything you wouldn't mind being broadcast on the radio. And remember, the longer you remain in a gossiper's company, the easier it becomes for you to share the details of your life and other people you know.

So what happens when you receive information from a gossiper?

You'll need to determine whether you'll accept their information as *your* truth. Exercise due diligence to ensure the information you receive is factual. Investigate. Interview. Ask questions.

If you act on the information and it turns out to be false, you might incite significant interpersonal conflicts and/or damage your position and influence as a trustworthy leader. Remember, every story sounds good until you hear the other side.[1]

LEADERSHIP REFLECTION

Have you ever trusted a leader with intimate details of your life and he or she shared your information with others? How did it make you feel? How was the situation resolved?

Without sharing details, has there ever been a time when you accepted gossip as *your* truth, only to learn the information was false? If so, please explain.

TWENTY - FIVE
HEALTH

If you don't take care of yourself, how can you take care of others?

Many leaders are so focused on their work that they neglect their own well-being. They work long hours, sleep very little, have poor eating habits, and are virtually nonexistent among their friends and family.

Without the proper mental, physical, social, and spiritual health, you might find yourself weighed down with depression, stress, poor decisions, and illicit behavior. However, maintaining a healthy lifestyle will help you alleviate negative behaviors, extend your longevity, and keep your position and legacy as a leader intact.

Four Legs of Health[2]

Consider your mental, physical, social, and spiritual health as legs of a chair. To keep your chair from becoming unbalanced when you sit on it, each leg would have to be stable and even with the others in order to help you maintain a balanced and consistent standard of health (10).

1. Mental. Maintaining mental health is exercising the self-control to continually focus on the positive while dispatching negative thoughts. If you think on nothing but negativity, your body and actions will follow. Stress, depression, weight gain (or loss), and other ailments might manifest because of negative thinking.

But what would happen if you remain positive and optimistic? In the same manner, your body and actions would also follow. Consider these benefits of good mental health:[3]

    a. lower rates of depression;

    b. lower levels of distress;

    c. greater resistance to the common cold;

    d. better psychological and physical well-being;

    e. reduced risk of death from cardiovascular disease;

    f. better coping skills during hardships and times of stress;

    g. increases your life span.

2. Physical. Leadership requires emotional, mental, and social energy and effort. Similar to a battery, you might find yourself drained at the end of a long day or week.

You might not feel like eating healthy, talking to your family, or doing anything that doesn't require sitting in front of your television. Physical activity might become an afterthought.

However, an emphasis on greater physical activity would allow you to be more focused, less tired, and have greater productivity. When it comes to your physical health, there are some things you have no control over, such as your genetic makeup, but placing a greater emphasis on physical health might provide several benefits:[4]

> a. controls your weight;
>
> b. reduces your risk of cardiovascular disease;
>
> c. reduces your risk for type 2 diabetes and metabolic syndrome;
>
> d. reduces your risk of some cancers;
>
> e. strengthens your bones and muscles;
>
> f. improves your mental health and mood;
>
> g. improves your ability to do daily activities and prevent falls, if you're an older adult;
>
> h. increases your chances of living longer;
>
> i. helps you sleep better.

3. Social. As you network, meet people, collaborate, and counsel, you pour out so much of yourself that you need

social relationships that pour back into you. You need people in your life you can vent to, be honest with, laugh with until your sides hurt, and just be yourself.

Meeting a friend for lunch, calling a mentor, going on vacation with your family, and inviting friends over for game night are a few ways you can connect socially. These intentional social connections help you recharge your batteries so you can continue leading and serving effectively.

4. Spiritual. Unfortunately, you might have to face tragic situations and events. Spiritual health can help instill the internal fortitude, perseverance, quiet assurance, and confidence you need to weather difficult and challenging situations (35). Sometimes, the spiritual health you have might be the encouragement, comfort, or support someone else needs to get through his or her own difficult season.

As you seek a healthy balance in your life, you must also emphasize the same for your followers. They often neglect their own mental, physical, social, and spiritual health in order to receive your acceptance and approval. They want to be considered hard working and loyal; supporters of your vision, mission, and direction. And because they might have less control over their schedules, they will require your intentional engagement and promotion to encourage healthier mental, physical, social, and spiritual lifestyles.

LEADERSHIP REFLECTION

If you sat in your health *chair*, would all four legs remain flat on the floor, or would the chair rock back and forth because of an imbalance? Please explain.

What area(s) of your mental, physical, social, or spiritual health require the greatest attention? Please explain.

How can you begin balancing your mental, physical, social, and spiritual health?

TWENTY - SIX
HELP

Help is a two-way street.

Leadership is not all about what you can get from your followers; it's also how you can help them. Your position often affords you the opportunity and ability to share your time, talent, resources, and money. You often have the means to make work a little easier, relieve stress, help others achieve a personal or professional goal, or provide financial assistance (42).

Time

Each of us receives 1,440 minutes each day (48). Some people make good use of their time and others do not. But if you consider how you can best use your minutes to help someone in need, you have an opportunity to make a huge investment in someone's life.

Who was the person who taught you how to ride a bike or drive a stick shift?

What friend helped you through an extremely difficult season of your life?

You remember these moments and the people who helped you vividly. These individuals freely gave their time to help you. Their investment left an impressionable mark in your life that might never be erased.

Talent

A talent is a special or natural ability or aptitude. I'd like to think that everyone has at least one talent. However, when many people think of a talent, they might consider it in terms of what can be monetized or used for greater popularity and success. But not every talent can (or should) be used in this manner.

Whatever your talent might be, I'd like to challenge you to consider how you can use your talent without monetizing it or seeking greater popularity or success. You never know when someone you meet will desperately need what you've been created and gifted to do, but cannot afford what you would charge.

Resources

Resources are considered a stock or supply of materials, staff, and other assets that a person or organization can use to function effectively. As a leader of a group or organization, you might have many available resources. Through your associations and networks, you might have the resources to help others meet their needs and reach their goals (7, 33).

Money

If you research some of the wealthiest men and women in the world, many of them give large portions of their wealth to help others. They use money as a means to create opportunities, meet specific needs, and fulfill desires. Through their giving, they inspire hope for a better and brighter tomorrow and open doors that many believed were closed. But you don't have to be rich to inspire hope or open doors.

No matter how small or large your financial contribution might be, you can make a difference in someone's life. You could provide a meal for a family, capital to start a business, tuition to continue a college education, rent to prevent an eviction, or even a suit or dress for a job interview. These acts of compassion and generosity give people hope that their tomorrow can be better than today—dreams can become a reality (15).

Helping others often provides meaning, purpose, and opportunities for many people (42). When you see needs that require a bit of time, talent, resources, or money, consider giving your best to meet these needs (1). You'll not only be a blessing to those you help, but yourself as well. Helping others makes you feel good. It lets you know you still have much to offer the world.

LEADERSHIP REFLECTION

Describe a situation when someone freely gave his or her time, talent, resources, or money to help you.

Considering time, talent, resources, or money, which have you been the most apprehensive to share? Please explain.

Describe some of the immediate needs for help that currently exist among your followers, organization, and local community.

TWENTY-SEVEN
HUMILITY

Leaders are given positions of greater authority and responsibility. Sadly however, some leaders have allowed pride to negatively influence the execution of their positions. These leaders grow increasingly selfish and create toxic environments that stifle growth, camaraderie, or any type of collaboration. At any and all costs, they work to build their own *kingdoms*, demanding to be served rather than supporting, serving, and appropriately leading those within their care.

Humility, on the other hand, is a modest or low view of your own importance or standing. But humility should never be considered as a sign of weakness. A person who displays humility actually exercises greater self-control and strength. Any person can yell, be angry, and boss people around, but how many can control his or her emotions in the midst of difficult circumstances, treat others equally without regard to position or status, and celebrate the accomplishments of a rival?

When you have a modest or low view of your own importance, you're not devaluing who you are as a person or a leader. Humility keeps you from abusing your positions of greater authority and responsibility. It helps you resist pride and selfishness so you can appropriately guide, support, and care for those you lead.

LEADERSHIP REFLECTION

Have you ever worked for a superior who lacked humility? If so, please describe how you and others within his or her area of responsibility was impacted.

Have you ever struggled to remain humble when given positions of greater authority and responsibility? If so, please explain how.

How can humility help you lead more effectively?

T W E N T Y - E I G H T
HUMOR

Laughter is medicine for the soul.[5]

As you often set the tone and environment for your group or organization, it might be important to ensure your followers have opportunities to laugh and relax from time to time. Fun, laughter, and other group activities are important for relieving stress and increasing group camaraderie.

When engaging in humor, you should ensure it's used with consideration for others within specific boundaries (16, 38). Some groups and organizations allow sarcastic banter and practical jokes in order to create a more *relaxed* working environment. However, you must ensure everyone in your group or organization approves of this *standard* because at some point, each person could become the topic of conversation. If everyone is not in agreement, sarcastic banter and practical jokes might become *weapons* to embarrass, insult, or intimidate rather than increase camaraderie. Therefore, before your group or organization enjoys a few laughs, ensure everyone plays by the *rules* so you can minimize the potential of anyone becoming embarrassed, insulted, or intimidated.

LEADERSHIP REFLECTION

Describe the most humorous group or organization you've been a part of.

Have any of your followers ever become embarrassed, insulted, or intimidated through the use of sarcastic banter and practical jokes? If so, what steps did you take to rectify the situation?

In what ways can you incorporate humor in your areas of responsibility? What would you need to consider before proceeding?

T W E N T Y - N I N E
INNOVATION

The beauty of leading others is that each person is a collection of thoughts, ideas, talents, and experiences separate from your own. Each person has a different perspective on how he or she views and interacts with the world. Because of this *uniqueness*, you might have an opportunity to create a culture of innovation; to solve challenging problems and create new plans, processes, and products. In order to capitalize on this opportunity, please consider the following within your team environment:

1. You're not the only person with good ideas. Many leaders believe their position entitles them to be the sole source of innovation and the only ideas that can be implemented are their own. Whether you realize it or not, you might have some highly intelligent and talented people around you. Someone on your team might have a better plan, process, or product than what you propose. Be humble enough to admit this and move on (27).

2. People willing to provide innovative ideas show they care. These individuals are displaying a vested interest in

your team and organization. They're doing more than just coming to work. They want to see improvements just as you do. Be ready and willing to listen. Provide an environment for them to share and work through their ideas as well as take on innovative projects.

3. Age, seniority, and position does not disqualify someone from having a good idea. The youngest or lowest-paid person on your team could have the most innovative idea among you all. Don't allow anyone's outward appearance, status, or position to discourage your consideration (16). Great ideas can come from the most unsuspecting people. You'd be amazed at what you can receive when you value each person's ideas.

4. Test new ideas and limits. Again, provide your team with the environment to share and work through their ideas freely without micromanaging them. Empower your team and allow them to have the physical space, resources, and time to devote to innovation (21).

5. Don't crush bad ideas. There are times when people share some crazy ideas, and there's no way you could implement them (as is). But their ideas could be a few iterations away from greatness. So instead of crushing their ideas, find other ways to either help them with further research and development or present their ideas before the entire team for additional consideration and collaboration (13).

Because these individuals care about their idea and involvement in the group or organization, they might be more sensitive to criticism. Be cognizant of their temperament and involvement on your team. Continue to encourage and include them as stakeholders. Allow them to share a role in the team's innovation and future growth.

6. Communicate, communicate, communicate (14). To innovate, you must communicate. Create an environment that allows each team member to provide honest and constructive feedback. Ensure different perspectives can be freely shared.

7. Coach and cheerlead. As your team begins to cultivate various ideas, lead from the sidelines as a coach and cheerleader to encourage, support, and provide guidance when and where needed. This might be the catalyst for your team to develop greater problem-solving skills, inspire more innovative ideas, increase personal pride and commitment, and provide an environment for shaping future leaders.

LEADERSHIP REFLECTION

Have you ever had an innovative idea that your leaders didn't accept? If so, please explain. How did you feel about their decision?

What has been the greatest challenge for innovation on your team or in your organization? What steps would you suggest taking to change this?

If you have led an innovative project for your group or organization, provide details on how you led your team and how the opportunity shaped your leadership abilities.

T H I R T Y
INTEGRITY

Integrity is the bedrock of leadership.

Integrity is the quality of being honest and having strong moral principles. It's the internal fortitude to do what's right, even when no one's looking (22). Having integrity means making the right decision that seems hard to make and doing the right thing because it's the right thing to do.

Integrity is similar to trust (49). Like trust, integrity can be lost in an instant, but it doesn't take years to build integrity within a team or organization. Integrity is expected from day one.

Whatever job, task, or assignment a leader is given, there's an expectation that he or she will carry it out in an absolute and resolute manner. If someone is babysitting, the parent(s) expect the child(ren) will be treated appropriately and cared for. If someone is leading a candy drive, there's an expectation that he or she will not eat the candy (without paying for it first) and will ensure all money collected is accounted for and submitted to the proper organization. If leading an organization, a leader is expected to embody the principles of the organization and serve with honest, unbiased, and uncompromising character (12).

LEADERSHIP REFLECTION

How have you incorporated integrity into your personal and professional lives?

What types of challenges have you faced in remaining a person of integrity?

If the integrity of someone you know was compromised, how did he or she recover? What was your role in his or her life during that period?

T H I R T Y - O N E
LIFELONG LEARNING

After years of public school (college, etc.), the last thing many people want to do is read or study. However, in leadership, there's a great benefit in being a lifelong learner.

Each person is a collection of his or her education, decisions, and experiences. Each one shapes his or her perspective on the people, plans, and processes they engage and lead on a daily basis. Lifelong learning allows each person to further expand his or her knowledge, perspective, and leadership capacity in order to positively impact people, plans, and processes toward a specific goal or purpose.

1. Read and study. Some people read local or national news and professional journals, take college courses, or read a book each month. Based on your profession, hobby, or other interests, a vast collection of information is available in libraries, across the Internet, and in bookstores.

2. Be deliberate. Become knowledgeable on current issues and topics personally or professionally relevant to you and your group or organization. Study specific topics that help you further develop the major areas of your life, not only leadership and business.

3. Share. As a leader, you'll have daily opportunities to speak to small and large groups of people. Be a conduit of information. Freely share what you've learned.

4. Encourage lifelong learning. Within your areas of responsibility, there are leaders all around you (everyone is a leader). Use your personal interactions to not only share information but to encourage lifelong learning. Provide programs and resources to help them expand their knowledge, perspective, and leadership capacity.

LEADERSHIP REFLECTION

How has lifelong learning impacted your personal and professional development?

In what ways can you encourage others to be lifelong learners?

How are you educating yourself today?

THIRTY - TWO
MENTORING

Mentoring is the passing of specific information or abilities from an experienced and trusted advisor to someone who is less experienced. Mentoring can occur anywhere, at any time, and by anyone. Mentoring can be as simple as showing a child how to tie his or her shoes, ride a bike, or navigate through a difficult subject in school.

Mentoring is a personal investment of time, talent, resources, and even money. This investment often occurs without fee or obligation to the one being mentored. It comes through a desire to improve the life of another person, no matter how large or small.

Before you share any information with your mentee, you should both communicate the intent of the mentoring experience, time constraints, limitations, and availability. This doesn't need to be a formal event, but there shouldn't be any misconceptions of expectations or deliverables.

As the focus of mentoring is on the mentee, it might be important for you to learn your mentee's preferred learning method. A mentee might be a visual, auditory, or tactile learner, and by using his or her preferred learning method, you might provide a more effective learning experience.

Mentoring, however, does require patience, understanding, and compassion (15, 26). Very few people are able to learn how to ride a bike on their first attempt. A little encouragement, support, and space for a mentee to make mistakes and work through his or her *process* can go a long way in his or her development.

Mentoring is your opportunity to share your knowledge, information, and expertise. Mentoring is a tremendous honor; someone considers you an experienced and trusted advisor who can help him or her learn and grow. Please don't take these opportunities for granted.

LEADERSHIP REFLECTION

What mentor has made the greatest impact in your life? Please share one or two examples.

If you were a mentor to another person, describe how you shared your knowledge, information, and expertise.

THIRTY - THREE
NETWORKING

Networking represents personal or professional connections with individuals and groups that periodically exchange or provide time, talent, resources, or money toward a specific purpose or goal. Networking is similar to collaboration as connections and communities form the foundation of networks. However, the difference in networking is that these connections and communities do not work together to accomplish a specific or common goal. Each connection or community works independently of the requestor, often using their own connections and communities to achieve the requestor's specific purpose or goal.

In order to develop sound networking connections and communities, please consider the following:

1. Build good connections and communities. Take a moment to review chapter thirteen, Collaboration. Chapter thirteen covers the basis for forming connections and communities, which are established through shared interests, abilities, and associations within personal and professional relationships.

2. Be a team player. Networking is a two-way street. Just as you would like to receive someone's time, talent, resources, or money, he or she might request the same from you one day.

3. Cultivate your connections. Some leaders rarely communicate with their connections or communities unless they need something. Take the initiative to contact them when you don't have a specific request. Stop by their office, send an e-mail, make a phone call, or reach out via social media. If necessary, build recurring reminders on your calendar to remind you to contact your connections or communities in specific or alternating intervals.

LEADERSHIP REFLECTION

How has networking improved your personal and professional lives?

What has been your most difficult challenge in networking with others?

T H I R T Y - F O U R
PERCEPTION

Perception often becomes reality...

Perception is an assumption of a particular item, person, or situation void of any facts. Although the assumption might actually be true, it's important for leaders to assess, make decisions, and lead based on truthful information. If you choose to lead by assumption, you could compromise your credibility, trustworthiness, and competency as a leader.

Combat perception with truth.

Before you commit to any decision or action, uncover as much information as you can about a particular item, person, or situation. If something sounds too good to be true, it might be, but find out by doing your due diligence to uncover the truth (24). If you cannot prove something to be true, leave it out of your communication until you can prove its validity (14).

On the flip side of perception, there will be many people that will have varying perceptions of you. Some will be true. Some will be false. However, many of these people will not try to determine whether the information they receive is true or false, they will accept it *as is* and allow it to become *their* reality.

You can spend your days trying to prove each person wrong, or you can live and lead by example (22). You can allow your actions to speak louder than another person's perception of you, combatting their assumptions with *your* truth.

You can't control what anyone will think or say about you, but you can control what you think, what you say, and how you conduct yourself. Regardless of what anyone perceives you to be, dedicate yourself to being a leader of integrity and truth. Allow your truth to become *their* reality.

LEADERSHIP REFLECTION

Have you ever made a decision based on perception? What was the outcome of your decision?

Has a negative perception of you interfered with your ability to lead others? What steps (if any) have you taken to address this situation?

THIRTY - FIVE
PERSEVERANCE

Perseverance is the mental, physical, social, and spiritual resolve to progress toward a purpose or goal in spite of hardships or challenging circumstances. In leadership, you might face situations that cause you to become frustrated, discouraged, or ready to quit or give up. In those moments, perseverance provides the fortitude to face, endure, and overcome hardships or challenging circumstances.

The negative emotions, feelings, and desires you experience during hardships or challenging circumstances might be evidence that your resolve is low. When your resolve is high, you might still experience these emotions, feelings, and desires, but you would be able to persevere in spite of them. However, when your resolve is low, it can feel like a ton of bricks is weighing you down.

One of the best ways to strengthen your resolve is to place a greater focus on your mental, physical, social, and spiritual health (25). Maybe you'll need to spend some time alone, write in your diary or journal, watch television, exercise, spend time with family and friends, or seek spiritual guidance and advice. Hopefully in time, your outlook will become increasingly positive, and you'll feel more capable of facing, enduring, and overcoming the hardships and challenges before you.

Sometimes it's OK not to be OK, but it's not OK to stay *there*. At some point, you'll face hardships or challenging circumstances, but they don't have to stifle or end your progress. Allow them to become stepping-stones toward reaching your purpose or goal. You can endure and overcome. Don't give up. Keep fighting the good fight.

LEADERSHIP REFLECTION

Share an example of how perseverance has helped you face, endure, or overcome a hardship or challenging circumstance.

What activities help you strengthen your resolve?

T H I R T Y - S I X
PERSONAL TOUCHES

Personal touches are genuine acts of kindness that have a positive impact on a person, group, or organization. Each act represents an intentional commitment of time, talent, resources, or money in order to inspire, encourage, or show appreciation (20).

Personal touches can be as simple as handwriting cards to acknowledge a significant moment in a team member's life, conducting office visits, or hosting a dinner to show your appreciation for your team's hard work. Personal touches should be varied and specific to each situation and person, group, or organization, but the same (or similar) act should be available to all. You must consider the precedent any personal touch might set because if you do something for one person, you must be willing to do the same for all (35). If you fail to consider this, your acts could be viewed as favoritism rather than acts of sincere kindness—even if you had the best intentions (34).

Any number of personal touches are meaningless without sincerity. Writing letters, personal visits, and dinners don't mean much to others when they know you're just going through the motions like a robot.

Some people will respond positively to personal touches. Others might not. But regardless of any person's response, allow your personal touches to speak volumes of your character and conduct as a leader (12).

LEADERSHIP REFLECTION

Describe the most memorable personal touch you've received.

What personal touches can you use to inspire, encourage, or show appreciation for your those in personal and professional lives?

PLEASE AND THANK-YOU

Proper etiquette and professional conduct is an expectation for those in leadership. Demonstrating proper etiquette and professional conduct is displaying behaviors that are mindful of your surroundings and considerate of those in your company (16). Because we all come from different backgrounds and cultures, we might not always learn about various *rules* of proper etiquette and professional conduct. Below are a few *rules* for you to consider in public and private settings:

1. Introductions. Be the first to extend your hand for a handshake. Ensure your grip is firm but not crushing, and definitely not limp or clammy. Maintain eye contact throughout your greeting. Remember to smile.

2. Communication. Use sir, ma'am, or official positions and titles when addressing those you meet. If the individual would like to be addressed differently, he or she will tell you. Make proper eye contact when talking. Remain engaged without looking at your watch or

answering your phone (unless you're expecting an important call).

When speaking in an official capacity, minimize your use of slang, and don't be loud or unruly. This includes when you're talking on your phone.

When answering your phone, you never know who might call you, so have an appropriate greeting. Be aware of your posture and body language when talking on the phone. Your tone will reflect your body language.

3. Meetings. Provide an introduction, summary, and conclusion for each meeting. If you're meeting a subordinate and the topic of your meeting is to direct or discipline, remain seated behind your desk when he or she walks in. If you're meeting a subordinate and the topic of your meeting is to encourage or mentor, stand when he or she enters your office, and move from behind your desk. If your office allows, sit next to him or her rather than remaining behind your desk. Before your meeting concludes, summarize the conversation and outline any necessary takeaways or tasks.

4. Public settings. Be on time (48). If you're going to be more than fifteen minutes late, contact the host. Respect personal space. Open doors for others. When sitting in tight or crowded areas, offer your seat to the elderly, pregnant women, people with many children, and others who might be injured or sick.

114

Be polite. People might have a negative attitude or demeanor, but you never know what they're going through. Instead of getting upset and escalating the situation, it might be best to let it go and walk away. This doesn't excuse their behavior, but it could prevent an unfortunate or senseless event from occurring.

If you accidentally bump into someone, be quick to apologize, and if something was dropped, help pick it up.

5. Eating at formal events. After general greetings, stand behind your chair until the event begins, all attendees assigned to your table arrive, or you're directed to sit. Sit down and rise from your chair on the right side. Do not slouch in your chair.

In most scenarios involving a formal place setting, forks will be placed on the left.[6] Work them from the outside in: salad fork and dinner fork. On the right, you might have your dinner knife, teaspoon, and soup spoon. Your bread plate and knife are on the upper left, dinner plate is in the middle, and your water is on the right. Your dessert fork and spoon might be placed above your dinner plate.

Wait until everyone has been served before eating your food. If the delay is long, wait until the host acknowledges when you can begin eating. Sometimes when the delay is too long, someone who has not been served at your table might ask for those who have been served to begin eating.

Don't reach over another person to retrieve something on the table (e.g., sugar, salt/pepper). Ask someone who is closer to pass the item to you. Unless directly asked for a specific item, pass other items such as the bread basket or salad dressing counterclockwise (to the right).

While eating, having your wrists on the table is fine, but not your elbows. Bring food to your mouth rather than lowering your head to the plate. Don't talk with food in your mouth. Don't smack or make noises while eating or drinking.

If you need to leave the table, cross your fork and knife on the plate, excuse yourself quietly, and set your napkin loosely on your chair.

When you've finished eating, place your napkin to the left of your plate and your fork and knife at the eleven o'clock position on the dinner plate. If you drink coffee or tea, place your spoon on the bottom left of the coffee or tea plate when you no longer require its use.[7]

LEADERSHIP REFLECTION

How has proper etiquette and professional conduct helped you in public or private settings?

How do you view people with poor etiquette or unprofessional conduct?

Please share any additional *rules* of proper etiquette or professional conduct that were not mentioned in this chapter.

THIRTY - EIGHT
PRECEDENT

A precedent is any act or decision case that serves as a guide or justification for subsequent acts or decisions. Every day, leaders make decisions that establish various precedents in their areas of responsibility. However, many leaders might not understand or consider the second- and third-order effects of their decisions.

For example, you host a *special* office luncheon at your home for one of your subordinates who is departing the organization. As the attendees enjoyed the luncheon, every person who departs from then on will probably expect the same type of luncheon. This is setting a precedent.

Though you provided a *personal touch* for a subordinate, you must understand how your decisions might establish certain expectations or standards (36). What would happen if several people departed from your organization without receiving a *special* office luncheon? How do you imagine they would feel?

Each person you lead expects you to treat everyone equally, give similar opportunities to all, provide fair and consistent discipline, and make decisions without bias. So before you do or say anything that will affect your group or organization, consider this one question:

If I do this for one, can I realistically do it for all?

LEADERSHIP REFLECTION

Have you ever—intentionally or unintentionally—established a precedent that couldn't be sustained or had a negative impact on your group or organization? If so, please explain.

THIRTY-NINE
PROBLEM-SOLVING

A leader is often a focal point for solving problems. Some problems are work related, and others might be personal. Whether or not a problem is work related, its effects can spread across every aspect of an individual's personal or professional life. It has the potential of negatively impacting his or her effectiveness or conduct and your group dynamic. Therefore, it's important to proactively address problems as they arise rather than allowing them to linger and grow into larger and more impactful issues.

When faced with problems, please consider the following ways you might address them within your areas of responsibility:

1. Delegate (21). Empower your managers and supervisors to assist you in solving problems at their levels of assignment. Share your direction and guidance and provide training when needed. Address problems that are so unique or challenging that only you can (or should) resolve them or your managers and supervisors could not reach a resolution.

For problems that reach your level, it's best to address them when they have recently surfaced or as soon as you become aware of them (11). If some issues are not addressed in a timely manner, other symptoms of the problem might also arise.

2. Address the problem. Understand that as you approach various problems, each person involved wants to *win*. Every individual wants to ensure that his or her needs, wants, and desires are not only heard but met. Few people are coming to give you what you want. They want what they want.

In problem-solving, one of your major goals is to reach the source of the problem. With getting to the source, you should first seek to understand the problem (19). Learn as much as you can from each person involved so you'll have a better understanding of the problem, the perspective of each person involved, any impacts the problem might have caused, and the desired solution or outcome.

When a number of individuals are involved, if feasible, speak to each person alone before bringing them together as a group. This will allow you to hear each person's concerns separately without interruptions from any other member. (What a person says in private settings might be different from what he or she says in public.) If you're meeting in a private office, have a neutral third party in the room as a witness to the conversation.

3. Establish a group solution. After speaking with each person, bring them together. When you bring them

together, initiate a guided discussion (led by you) and establish rules of conduct. Because you have people with varying intentions, motives, and emotions involved, some will want to avoid, accommodate, compete, compromise, or collaborate. Rules of conduct will ensure each person is allowed to freely and respectfully share his or her concerns without belittling or attacking another person or being belittled or attacked.

After each person has had an opportunity to share his or her concerns, summarize their comments. This might be an appropriate time to share your own unbiased thoughts. Your view should be from a perspective that provides greater clarity and insight, not one that forces the group to decide on a specific course of action...unless it's warranted. If a solution is agreed upon, if necessary, establish a timeline for implementation. If the group cannot come to an agreed solution, schedule another meeting and repeat these steps as necessary.

Problem-solving is a delicate art that will change with each person and/or situation you face. With a bit of patience and good communication skills, you'll be off to a great start for solving problems and moving your group and organization forward (14).

LEADERSHIP REFLECTION

What has been your greatest challenge in problem-solving?

What additional warnings or advice would you give for solving problems?

Share one of your greatest successes in problem-solving.

F O R T Y
PUBLIC SUCCESS
PRIVATE FAILURE

Are you the same person in private that you are in public?

For many leaders, the answer is *no*—they live very different lives.

In public, some leaders are considered visionaries, compassionate, brilliant, humble, hardworking, and successful. But if you speak to those who know them in private—that is, family and close friends—you might hear a different account: impatient, absent, abusive (verbally, emotionally, or physically), ungrateful, or hypocritical.

Many leaders invest a lot of their time and energy on who they are in the public spotlight. They give the very best of themselves for people who know the least about them. However, leadership is both a public and private matter.

Your character in public should be an extension of who you are in private (12). Live a life that those in public and private settings can admire.

LEADERSHIP REFLECTION

What would the people who see your private life say about you?

What comes to mind when you think about the statement, "Your private life can overshadow your life's greatest achievements?"

How can you bring greater balance to your public and private lives?

FORTY - ONE
PUNCTUALITY

Punctuality is the strict observance of being on time and prompt to meetings, appointments, and other scheduled events. As there are no refunds once seconds tick away, it's important to make the best use of your time and respect other people's time by being punctual (47).

Whether you're the organizer of an event or an attendee, punctuality represents two things: being prepared and departing your location with enough time to arrive early. Being prepared can represent a number of qualitative factors, such as time and calendar management, ironing your clothing the day prior, setting your alarm clock to wake up early, having all of your materials in one place, and leaving early enough to arrive a few minutes early (48). It's better to arrive fifteen or twenty minutes early than five minutes late.

If you're hosting a meeting, begin and end on time. Unless you're waiting for a very important attendee, respect those who arrived on time.

If you don't respect your meeting times, why should your attendees? If you establish a precedent of starting and ending late, punctuality will not be a concern and your attendees might not respect the time of anyone but themselves (38).

If your meeting gets close to the scheduled end, you have the option of scheduling another meeting to continue the discussion at a later date or time. By doing this, you ensure that your stance on punctuality is intact while meeting the needs of your audience and key decision-makers.

LEADERSHIP REFLECTION

How do you feel when people are not punctual to your meetings, appointments, and other scheduled events?

Share your methods for arriving to your meetings, appointments, and other scheduled events on time.

F O R T Y - T W O
PURPOSE

Purpose is the reason something is done or used; a feeling of being determined to do or achieve something; a person's aim or goal.

When many people think about purpose, they often think about the one thing they were placed on this earth to do— their life's purpose. Some people might know what their life's purpose might be and others have yet to discover theirs.

Hopefully, your thoughts, words, and decisions will one day lead you to find your life's purpose. Waiting to discover your life's purpose doesn't mean your life currently has less meaning or value. Your life already has great value and you can greatly contribute to those around you.

Everyday you can live a life with purpose, on purpose. Every opportunity, experience, and situation is an opportunity to be determined, give your best effort, and accomplish your goals (1). Purpose is not only what you do. It's a mind-set that makes up who you are.

Think about it. If you're a street sweeper, you can clean the streets so well that people can eat off them. At that moment, your work defines your purpose of being. Your work product defines who you are and what you're capable of producing. It also shows your commitment to your craft and duty performance (22).

Use each moment of your life as an opportunity to live with purpose, on purpose, and to inspire those around you. You never know what doors might open as a result.

LEADERSHIP REFLECTION

What does it mean for you to live each day with purpose, on purpose? Provide specific examples.

F O R T Y - T H R E E
ROUTINES

Leaders can be pulled in many different directions on a daily basis. People want their advice, approval, mentorship, etc. all day...everyday. With so many people to speak with and issues to address, it's easy for leaders to move from one hot issue to another without any sense of control or direction.

Now, I do believe you should make yourself available to your people and organization, but I also believe you can implement routines that allow you to complete specific responsibilities or tasks on a scheduled and systematic basis. Routines can help you create specific methods for being more productive, focused, and balanced.

Do you have a morning routine to start your day?

Do you set aside specific times during your day, week, or month to work on important projects and specific tasks?

Keep routines simple and not so complicated or unrealistic that you can't sustain them for long periods. Ensure your routines are flexible enough to handle unexpected interruptions. This will allow you to address any interruptions and return to your routine without your entire day being *ruined*.

LEADERSHIP REFLECTION

Take a few moments to consider how you can establish routines to help you get the most from your 1,440 minutes each day.

FORTY-FOUR
SELF-AWARENESS

Self-awareness empowers you with the knowledge of your thoughts, mannerisms, and behaviors in a given situation. Based on what you know and learn about yourself, you'll know to stay clear of specific individuals or groups and refrain from participating in certain conversations. You'll also know your most optimal times of productivity or when you need to take a break. And more importantly, you might prevent irreparable damage to your good name, character, or positions of leadership.

Total self-awareness is not something you come to learn about yourself in a single moment. Many of us spend a lifetime learning little details about ourselves. There will be things you'll like about yourself, and many other traits you wish you never knew about.

Self-awareness is about honesty, openness, and exposure. Don't lie to yourself to protect your own self-image or create an environment where honesty, openness, and exposure cannot exist.

Take time during your day or week to assess your thoughts, mannerisms, behaviors, weaknesses, and temptations. Incorporate this assessment into your RESET (10). For example, consider or describe your:

a. choice of words in personal interactions;

b. behavior in times of frustration or anger;

c. personal thoughts during specific meetings or scenarios;

d. decisions you made and your motives behind them.

As you gain greater self-awareness, your standards and boundaries should adjust accordingly, and your *yes* and *no* should become more defined (10, 46, 50).

LEADERSHIP REFLECTION

What has been the most difficult part of assessing your behavior and conduct?

How has self-awareness benefited you as a leader?

FORTY-FIVE

SERVICE

To lead is to serve.

Leaders are often in the best position to serve. They have the necessary authority and accountability to incorporate themselves into their areas of responsibility (2, 9). Sadly however, many leaders use their positions to be served rather than using service as a means to support, connect with, and care for others (26). As you lead your group or organization, please consider the following four aspects of service:

1. Know your subordinates. What would happen if you took the time to learn more about your subordinates? What you might discover is that many of your subordinates are dealing with challenges you never fathomed were possible. When you're at work, you see happy and smiling faces, but some of them might be worried about losing their home, feeding their children, or hoping their car doesn't break down.

2. Fulfill requests. Learning about those you serve might give you an opportunity to meet some of their needs. You

might not be able to solve every issue, but there might be some issues that are within your ability to address.

As the leader, you might have the ability to release them early from work, sponsor an office lunch, take out the trash, deliver the office mail, provide a lawnmower to cut overgrown grass, or perform some other helpful task. Allow compassion, consideration, and personal touches to be your motivation for providing the most appropriate way you can serve others (15, 16, 36).

3. Be the example (22). Be willing to accomplish any task or assignment your subordinates perform. <u>Nothing</u> should be beneath you. Lead by example, not position. Allow your service to speak volumes about your character and leadership.

4. Service begets service. When you genuinely serve others, they will often reciprocate by finding ways to serve you. This reciprocation allows for connections of camaraderie, loyalty, and trust to be forged on both personal and professional levels.

LEADERSHIP REFLECTION

What have you found to be the most difficult aspect of serving others as a leader?

In what ways can you serve your group and organization?

FORTY-SIX
SLIPPERY SLOPES

One of the most important reasons leaders should remain mentally, physically, socially, and spiritually healthy is that any imbalance can lead to blind spots and destructive behaviors (25). Blind spots can occur when you become less attentive to your energy and stress levels while working through the grind of leading people and organizations. Destructive behaviors often result from an increased lack of inhibitions—similar to consuming alcohol. The more a person drinks alcohol, the less conscious he or she becomes of socially acceptable behavior. With no internal filter on his or her words or actions, the individual might begin saying or doing things he or she normally wouldn't when sober. Slippery slopes work in the same manner.

Slippery slopes can occur anytime you don't hold true to your standards of integrity and professional conduct (30). A slippery slope can begin with a smile, a simple comment, hanging out with questionable people, or maybe lowering a standard or two. The slide begins very slowly and gains momentum without much fanfare or notice.

Through your initial acceptance, you might begin a repetitive process of overriding inhibitions and warnings telling you not to do or say a specific thing. So in order to combat slippery slopes, you'll need to incorporate standards and boundaries into every area of your life:

1. Standards. In your personal and professional interactions, you'll need to determine what standards you'll choose to live by—deep, internal principles that lead and guide you. This may be as simple as determining to treat all people fairly, not to cheat on a test, or take an unfair advantage. These principles might often stem from your childhood, organizational values, or religious beliefs.

2. Boundaries. As you establish your standards, boundaries will keep you within the parameters (and the appearance) of good conduct. Maybe you decide not to meet someone of the opposite sex alone or keep certain conversations and relationships focused only on business. Build your boundaries so that everyone around you understands where they lie, even without you having to deliberately point them out.

Having standards and boundaries can help ensure that your character, integrity, and legacy cannot be criticized or slandered. This allows for you to lead without distraction or disruption so you can effectively accomplish your responsibilities and tasks.

LEADERSHIP REFLECTION

Share an example of a leader who lost his or her position through a slippery slope. How could this have been avoided?

Describe the most difficult challenge you've faced when dealing with a slippery slope.

After reviewing your answers from chapter ten, in what major areas of your life will you need to establish more defined standards and boundaries? Describe how you can accomplish this in each area, along with any potential challenges or obstacles.

FORTY-SEVEN
THE GOLDEN RULE

Treat others as you want to be treated.

The golden rule should be your standard for how you treat every person, regardless of status, position, or social and financial standing. Being in a position of authority doesn't give you any right to mistreat others. Every person has value, every person is worthy of respect, and no one deserves to be treated as trash or as if he or she is not worthy of your time or attention.

Throughout your day, the one question you should ask yourself is whether or not you would want to be treated the way you just treated someone. Sometimes the answer to that question will be *no*. Then it'll be up to you to be humble enough to apologize and correct your conduct to match what you would want in a similar situation (27).

Maybe you would want someone to give you a second chance, not cut you off in traffic, speak kindly, be happy for you, and help you when you need it most. But sadly, we're often guilty of the opposite and treat others less kindly than we would treat ourselves.

You don't want to be treated badly, so please don't treat others badly. Keep the golden rule as part of your standard of conduct, and treat others the way you want to be treated.

LEADERSHIP REFLECTION

Share an example of how the golden rule benefitted someone in your organization.

From what you've seen, what attributes or character traits exist when the golden rule is absent in leadership?

In what ways can the golden rule help you as a leader today? Please share an example.

FORTY - EIGHT
TIME MANAGEMENT

Time management is the ability to use your time in an effective or productive manner. As a leader, it's important to properly manage your time. Some people ensure that every second of their 1,440 minutes each day is accounted for, others only manage specific blocks of time, and more than a few have no schedule or system in place. Those with no schedule or system often find themselves lacking the effectiveness or productivity to adequately fulfill their responsibilities and tasks.

In order to effectively fulfill your responsibilities and tasks, you should establish a time management system that's based around your personality, personal preferences, and personal and professional needs and goals (44). Your system should be simple and easy to maintain so that you don't stop using it after a few months—nothing too complex or cumbersome.

For example, if you're not comfortable using a computer program, maybe a paper calendar, daily planner, or even a sheet of paper might work for you. If you prefer using your smartphone, you can choose an online calendar or time-management app. You might even decide to keep a mental note of your meetings, appointments, and other scheduled events.

As you consider your meetings, appointments, and other scheduled events, consider incorporating extra time for traveling (and rest breaks) when needed. You don't want your schedule to be so rigid that you become frustrated if you're running late to a meeting or an emergency arises. Lastly, consider including time management into your RESET (10).

LEADERSHIP REFLECTION

What difficulties have you faced in managing your time? List any prior attempts and systems you've tried and why they didn't work for you.

F O R T Y - N I N E
TRUST

Trust is the foundation of leadership. Trust is about people believing what you say, having faith in what you'll do, and believing that where (and how) you lead them is right.

Trust is formed through public perception and actual conduct. The basis for these is founded on the expectation that you'll carry out your responsibilities faithfully, have integrity, and be trustworthy and honest (30).

You build trust through your day-to-day decisions and conduct within your connections and communities (13). Each decision and action can be used as a stepping-stone for building trust. It takes a long time to earn and build trust, and it can all be lost in an instant through one careless decision or action.

LEADERSHIP REFLECTION

Who is the person you trust the most? What makes you have so much trust in him or her?

Share an example of a leader who had your trust but lost it through his or her words or actions.

What have you done to build trust among your group and in your organization?

F I F T Y
YES AND NO

Each day you're confronted with many decisions. *Yes* to this. *No* to that. Each decision opens new doors and closes others. *Yes* and *no* provide powerful opportunities, and your decisions should not be made in haste or haphazardly, as each carries its own benefit or consequence.

Many believe saying *yes* to numerous opportunities provides them with acceptance, appreciation, and better opportunities in the future. Though you want to say *yes* to every opportunity, a consequence of *yes* can be your time, relationships, or even the ability to complete certain goals. On the flip side, saying *no* removes you from specific opportunities today, but can provide better ones tomorrow.

Consider the implications of your *yes* and *no*. Think about the second- and third-order effects of your choices. Think about the *yes* and *no* decisions that brought you to where you are today and consider how your responses will impact your life and those connected to you tomorrow.

LEADERSHIP REFLECTION

Was there a *yes* or *no* you gave in haste or haphazardly that you wish you could take back? If so, please explain.

As a leader, do you give your followers time to consider their *yes* or *no*?

CONCLUSION

It is my solemn hope and prayer that *Everyone Is a Leader: Fifty Practical Ways to Build Tomorrow's Leaders Today* has provided you with the essential tools and information to be an effective leader with good morals and sound character. This book was my opportunity to share a lifetime of leadership experiences. Though I didn't specifically mention myself or provide any personal stories or examples, my life is revealed throughout every chapter. I've learned many of these lessons through simple experiences and hard consequences. And I wrote this book with the hope that you can learn from my successes and failures and become the leader you always hoped to be.

You are a leader. Not having a formal position doesn't make you any less of a leader. There might be people following you, trusting you, and believing in you right now. No position, parking spot, or extra money...only people seeking help, support, and advice from you.

Lead well. Encourage. Inspire. Be the change you always hoped to see in the world.

ENDNOTES

1—Proverbs 18:17.

2—Air Force Instruction 90-506, *Comprehensive Airman Fitness (CAF)*. United States Air Force. 19 May 2016. http://static.e-publishing.af.mil/production/1/saf_mr/publication/afi90-506/afi90-506.pdf.

3—"Positive thinking: Stop negative self-talk to reduce stress." Mayo Clinic. 23 August 2016. http://www.mayoclinic.org/healthy-lifestyle/stress-management/in-depth/positive-thinking/art-20043950

4—"Physical Activity and Health." Center for Disease Control and Prevention. 20 May 2016. http://www.cdc.gov/physicalactivity/basics/pa-health/.

5—Proverbs 17:22.

6—"Formal Place Setting—How to Set a Table." Good Housekeeping. 14 August 2016. http://www.goodhousekeeping.com/food-recipes/party-ideas/a25997/formal-place-setting/.

7—"The Utensil Etiquette Your Parents Never Taught You." Huffington Post. 21 May 2016. http://www.huffingtonpost.com/2014/10/20/utensil-etiquette_n_6004682.html.

(com)mission™
PUBLISHING

www.commissionpubs.com
info@commissionpubs.com

www.ingramcontent.com/pod-product-compliance
Lightning Source LLC
Chambersburg PA
CBHW070809050426
42452CB00011B/1962